A Bouquet from the Met

A Bouquet from the Met

Flower Arrangements by Chris Giftos

at The Metropolitan Museum of Art

By Barbara Plumb

with Page Starzinger

Photographs by Alec Hemer

Harry N. Abrams, Inc., Publishers

With heartfelt thanks

to

LILA ACHESON WALLACE

(1889–1984)

for her love of flowers

and

overwhelming generosity,

which gave me the opportunity

to paint with my own palette

for the pleasure of all visitors to

The Metropolitan Museum of Art

Frontispiece:

A dramatic mix of purple agapanthus and calla lilies enlivens the Louis XV room of the Wrightsman Galleries.

Page 4:

A white marble statue by Daniel Chester French (c. 1919) serves as a backdrop for a spectacular assemblage of delphinium blossoms.

Editor: Elisa Urbanelli
Designer: Darilyn Lowe Carnes

Page 128: Photograph © 1988 The Metropolitan Museum of Art

Library of Congress Cataloging–in–Publication Data
Plumb, Barbara.
A bouquet from the Met : flower arrangements by Chris Giftos at the Metropolitan Museum of Art / by Barbara Plumb with Page Starzinger ; photographs by Alec Hemer.
p.   cm.
ISBN 0–8109–4015–9 (cloth)
1. Flower arrangement—New York (State)—New York.
2. Metropolitan Museum of Art (New York, N.Y.) 3. Giftos, Chris.
I. Giftos, Chris. II. Starzinger, Page. III. Title.
SB449.P585   1998
745.92—dc21   97–29897

Harry N. Abrams, Inc.
100 Fifth Avenue
New York, N.Y. 10011
www.abramsbooks.com

CONTENTS

INTRODUCTION *Barbara Plumb*

If of thy mortal goods thou art bereft,
And from thy slender store two loaves alone are left
Sell one, and with the dole
Buy hyacinths to feed thy soul . . .

—Sadi (Persian poet of the twelfth century)

THAT THE METROPOLITAN MUSEUM OF ART IS AMONG the greatest museums in the world is universally recognized. But what is known only to the fortunate people who have actually visited the Met, as it is affectionately called by New Yorkers, is that it is also a truly hospitable museum. To walk inside the Great Hall of the Metropolitan Museum, one of America's great public spaces, is to be greeted as you would expect to be in an elegant, palatial house: with extravagant bouquets of beautiful flowers in stone urns grandly scaled to the architecture. Visitors from near and far respond appreciatively to the unexpected floral welcome of heady scents and stunning colors.

Since September 1970, Chris Giftos, the museum's resident genius with fresh flowers, has been creating for the pleasure of the museum's five million visitors each year four overscaled bouquets in the niches of the Great Hall, as well as two planted islands and a towering arrangement above the central information desk. This gracious gift of floral bounty is special to the Metropolitan and the envy of museums everywhere.

In 1969 the late Lila Acheson Wallace, cofounder of *Reader's Digest*, trustee of the Metropolitan Museum, and passionate flower lover, gave the unique endowment that makes Giftos's artistry possible: fresh flowers in the Great Hall once a week in perpetuity. In the spirit of her bequest "to create alive and breathing floral art,"

9

Giftos conceived the idea for this book: designing flower arrangements to enliven many of the museum's best-loved galleries.

Though it would be too complex and expensive a project to make new arrangements throughout the museum on a regular basis, as he does each week in the Great Hall, Giftos couldn't resist the challenge of creating them just once and capturing them forever in stun-

ning photographs. His hope is to inspire and delight flower lovers as well as art connoisseurs. "What could be more exciting than complementing the finest art with beautiful flowers?" Giftos asks. "It is the best of nature and of man."

Giftos gleaned ideas for the arrangements in this book by studying the masterpieces in the Met's eighteen curatorial departments and discussing them with the curators in charge. Quite understandably, he felt daunted by the vastness of his self-assigned turf and the complexity of the task he had set for himself. No one had ever before attempted to create flower arrangements specifically for the particular spaces of the museum. With the many changes of scale and style in the arrangements made especially for this book, Giftos provides ideas to satisfy almost everyone's taste, from casual to formal.

As Manager of Special Events at the Metropolitan Museum, Giftos has had to live up to an impossibly difficult job description: to invent imaginative party settings that never repeat themselves. The galleries that are most often chosen for festive occasions are: The Temple of Dendur in The Sackler Wing, The Wrightsman Galleries, the Carroll and Milton Petrie European Sculpture Court, and The Charles Engelhard Court of The American Wing. For conjuring the instant fantasy required to transform these monumental spaces into exciting, welcoming party settings, Giftos relies on his sixth and seventh senses of showmanship and wit.

"The first party I was responsible for at the museum was a big reception for the 'Before Cortez' exhibition," Giftos recalls. "The very day I started my new job, I had to transform the former Fountain Restaurant into the swamps of Xochimilco in Mexico. I waded into the fountain, wearing Bermuda shorts and sneakers, and made a forty-by-eighty-foot arrangement."

Whether assembling floral bouquets in the Great Hall, masterminding a glittering dinner party for five hundred distinguished guests, or orchestrating the choices for this book, Giftos sticks to his guiding principles: symmetry and harmony. "It is all math," he says matter-of-factly. "I choose five to eight different types of flowers and fifty to eighty stems for the Great Hall niche bouquets. Everything has to balance." The working time for creating one of these arrangements, once all the material has been gathered, is about an hour.

The unusually large-scale bouquets required by the Metropolitan's Great Hall seemed daunting to Giftos in the beginning, but they were nothing compared to the four-tiered, nine-foot-high arrangements he creates now. Calculating how long the many different varieties of flowers are going to last continues to challenge him. "I have to figure in my head which will grow together and die together," Giftos says. "Otherwise, I'd be on the ladder every single day. Also, I have to estimate which flowers will open around the same time."

For each of his large arrangements, Giftos makes a structure either with branches or greenery. "It is like building a house, with the foundation first," Giftos says. "The flowers start telling me where they belong. I work with one type of flower until I've finished with it and then go on to the next." Because he doesn't like his arrangements to look naked, he chooses stems "at the break," meaning they are no longer buds and are just starting to open. "As the buds begin to flower, a bouquet begins to change its face," Giftos says. Occasionally he selects only branches, such as quince, apple, or forsythia, "because they are so beautiful in their own right." He prefers the shape of his arrangements to be airy, open, and loose. "I want each flower to have the glory of being seen," he says. "If you stuff flowers into a bouquet, then you cannot see the individual stems. You have to give them room to breathe and grow."

Lila Acheson Wallace decreed that the museum's flower arrangements should be regal and splendid, appropriate for a modern-day equivalent of a royal palace. Her preference was for masses and masses of different varieties of blooms, and she asked Giftos to seek delicate yet interesting "special occasion" stems. In her opinion, the sumptuous arrangements in the Great Hall should be another act of consideration by the museum toward its visitors.

THESE FRESH FLOWERS ARE

THESE FRESH FLOWERS ARE
THE GENEROUS GIFT OF
THE GARDEN CLUB OF AMERICA

"Mrs. Wallace believed that being greeted by amazing fresh flowers soothes you, tranquilizes you," Giftos says, "and she wanted people to relax when they came to the Metropolitan." She envisioned the Great Hall as a gallery for displaying fresh flowers. She instructed Giftos, "You as much as any other curator have an exhibition going on, and the bouquets should be suitably large and grand."

"She took such joy in coming to see the flowers," Giftos recalls, "and she loved the letters of appreciation people wrote to her from all over the world. And she answered every single one."

Many of the flowers favored by Giftos for his arrangements are rare and sometimes imported. "People from all over the world come to this museum and they should see flowers they hardly ever have a chance to enjoy," he says. "Rare flowers go with rare art."

Each Thursday, he orders the stems from New York City suppliers, who fax or call in his requests to vendors in Holland. A careful and experienced shopper, Giftos is always on the lookout for sources that provide better quality at lower prices. Whether on the phone placing his orders or at the flower market buying, he is painting the Metropolitan Museum's bouquets in his head.

On Friday, his order is filled at the auctions in Holland. On Saturday, the flowers are flown to New York. They are delivered to the flower market, where Giftos picks them up early Monday morning. Later that day, while the Museum is closed to the public, he makes his arrangements in the Great Hall.

"I am married to the flowers until the following Sunday," Giftos says. "I have to check them every single day, taking dead ones out and replacing them with fresh ones. Sometimes the whole arrangement can collapse overnight, and I have to take it apart."

Typical of the exotic flowers Giftos might order in conjuring his floral wizardry are African Queen lilies, Casa Rosa lilies, and Vivaldi roses, which have green exteriors and pink interiors. "Whenever Mrs. Wallace would come, I always made sure to have blue delphiniums in at least one of my arrangements," Giftos recalls.

She loved blue. She owned blue diamonds; she wore blue dresses and suits. Picasso's *Blue Boy* hung over her mantelpiece. And one hill at her home in Mt. Kisco, New York, was covered in blue irises. She even wrote with blue ink on blue paper, which was decorated with a photograph of the house and the blue irises. On days when she visited, I wore a blue suit, blue shirt, and blue tie. And whatever presentation bouquet I gave her, I always remembered to tie it with blue ribbon.

Whenever Giftos decides to include Mrs. Wallace's favorite flowers—delphiniums—in an arrangement, he almost always combines them with rhubrum lilies and amaryllis lilies. He chooses lilies not only for their refinement and sophistication, but also for their long stems, which help them survive longer than any of his other favorites. "And they have a wonderful scent you can smell as soon as you walk into the Great Hall," he says.

Among the other flowers he orders frequently are French tulips. He is fascinated by the way they continue to grow another inch and a half to two inches while in the bouquet. Like all gardeners around the world, he delights in roses—colored in soft pastels, different shades of pink, and blue or white. "I seldom use red roses," Giftos says, "because the color is just too strong."

Peonies rank high on his list of preferred blooms, but they are only available a few weeks a year. "They have the shortest season of any of the flowers I work with," he says. He is also partial to dogwood, lilacs, tuberoses, freesia, azalea, euphorbia, and alstroemeria (also known as Peruvian lilies). When a new flower is introduced, he is sure to get it so that visitors to the Met may enjoy its beauty and novelty as soon as possible.

The skeleton of Giftos's arrangements is usually formed by one or several of his favorite branches, which include dogwood, quince, pear, corkscrew, willow, magnolia, rhododendron, and forsythia. To combat the inevitable post-Christmas blues, he uses yellow forsythia branches on their own. "In January," Giftos says, "people walk into the Great Hall out of the snow, take one look at the yellow forsythia, get smiles on their faces, and say, 'Well, spring cannot be that far off.'"

When mixing, contrasting, and blending colors in his arrangements, Giftos gets the same adrenaline rush as a painter experimenting with different pigments on a palette. "I feel a special thrill when I get very daring," he says. Giftos sees no reason not to be bold with color. After all, in the countryside there are no color juxtapositions that raise eyebrows or seem the slightest bit vulgar. An inveterate gardener, he knows from experience that the surprising combinations of hues found in nature often prompt one to say, "Why didn't I think of putting those colors together myself?"

Even though he may have a color theme in mind, Giftos has to balance that ideal against the reality of the marketplace. Even considering the enviable scope of his flower universe, he is limited by what is available on a certain week in a given season.

The classic gray stone urns that hold Giftos's flower arrangements have been fixtures in the Great Hall for some thirty years. They were specially designed to fit into the niches, which were originally created to display statues of women. Tradition keeps them there. No such precedent, however, has been set for the full-blown center bouquet above the information desk. Giftos can select any container he wishes for this arrangement. Among his choices are baskets, wine coolers, terra-cotta pots, and any number of other simple classic holders.

Given the restrictions on containers in the Great Hall, it's no wonder that Giftos warmed to the challenge of a book that gave him the freedom to select different types of vases and holders. "I feel the container is as important as the flowers," he says. "They have to complement each other. The flowers suggest the style to me."

Giftos recognizes as kindred spirits the floral painters whose works hang not only in the Metropolitan but in countless other museums around the world. The same essentials of color, proportion, texture, and scale that govern their work hold sway in the art of flower arranging as well.

Dutch painters first tried their hand at floral bouquets in the late sixteenth century. Their ravishing arrangements painted in oil on canvas, though not seasonally correct, still evoke a mood of reverie and recollection. Dark backgrounds make the ecstatically rendered blooms so radiant they almost seem capable of jumping off the canvas into a waiting vase. The otherworldly light, so typical of Dutch flower paintings, gives a radiance and luminosity to the blossoms. Abundant air around every stem allows each to be seen and savored for itself. Occasionally, household objects or fallen petals are included in the properly bourgeois settings, making them seem even more realistic.

During the nineteenth century, flower painting flourished in France. Redouté, Napoleon's court artist, was commissioned by the Empress Josephine to paint hundreds of portraits of her most prized roses in her beloved garden at Malmaison. Later in the century, Manet created urbane still lifes of lilacs and roses; Redon rendered bouquets with great exuberance and finesse; and Fantin-Latour painted flowers in a luminous, natural style.

It was the French Impressionists and Post-Impressionists who somehow managed to distill the very essence of flowers. Not just the color, texture, and contours but, intriguingly, the atmosphere, the scent, and, most spectacularly, the light. Monet is practically synonymous with his water lilies at Giverny, Van Gogh with his fluorescent yellow sunflowers in Provence. And who can resist the temptation to wallow in the gorgeous profusion of blooms by Cézanne and Bonnard, or savor the quiet, almost placid, bouquets of Degas and Vuillard? The sensual, passionate interpretations of flowers by these artists are particularly beloved.

Perhaps it is the power of natural beauty that accounts for the strong emotional attraction we feel to a glorious bouquet of flowers in a perfect container. But what compels us intellectually is the complex juggling of so many diverse elements. An arrangement must address the scale, color, texture, and form of stems, as well as their container, and then keep the composition in perfect balance with the surroundings in which it is displayed.

A large bouquet with its explosions of rich color and texture, and its strong formal outline softened with rakish swoops and bends of blooms or branches, is as key an element in a room as a striking piece of furniture or sculpture. More quiet and subtle but just as important are smaller arrangements whose role is not to arrest attention but to harmonize, like beautiful but discrete art objects.

Equal in significance to the relationship between the flowers and the surrounding space is that between the flowers and the container. With true synergy, the whole becomes greater than the sum of its parts. Too fussy or ornate a container can undo the harmony of this careful balancing act. As Giftos proves both in his large, loose arrangements and in his more modest, delicate ones, it is important that the container shows off the stems to their best advantage and allows each flower to be noticed and appreciated.

With all the art, artifice, sophistication, and money that goes into professional flower arranging today, it is fascinating to think that in Victorian times the lady or gentleman of the country house communicated to the head gardener what she or he had in mind for each room, and the gardener arranged the flowers as part of his job. In more modest domestic situations, the flower-arranging duties fell to mothers, aunts, or daughters, who prided themselves on their artistic skills. In these households, a knowledge of botany and horticulture was considered *de rigueur* for a properly educated child. (And, when you think about it, it was not exactly a quantum leap from reading Latin poetry and prose to learning Latin botanical names.) Well-bred young women of the time were steeped in an appreciation of nature and happily whiled away long, lazy afternoons painting watercolors of the flowers and plants they identified on their strolls. In those days, it would have been inconceivable for anyone with the right kind of manners to be ignorant of the names of the flowers that flourished in the surrounding meadows or that grew, carefully tended, in the cutting gardens.

Historically and culturally, flowers have played a part in every society. Flowers are one of the great phenomena of nature that have always fascinated human beings.

The ancient Chinese, who espoused the Confucian philosophy, which equates simplicity with beauty, tended toward the ascetic in flower display. Only one type of flower would be chosen for a bouquet, be it peonies, chrysanthemums, peach or plum blossoms, paper-white narcissus, or pine branches. Often one perfect stem in a container would be singled out as an object for contemplation, representing in microcosm the cycle of all life. To the Chinese eye, abundance was confusing; it was spiritually cloying to the soul.

In Japan as early as the twelfth century, a master of ikebana (the Japanese art of flower arranging) wrote that it was ill-advised to arrange flowers when feeling hostile, depressed, or anxious because an arrangement mirrors the soul. Even today, too much perfection in an arrangement bothers the Japanese. They like to see a slightly "off" touch, such as a quirky flash of color peeping forth or some bare blooms that remind them of those flowers in the garden that have lost their petals.

We are forever in the Egyptians' debt, as it was they who discovered the rose in the fourth century B.C. Evidence discovered in ancient tombs excavated in the Nile Valley suggests that the Egyptians were very sophisticated in designing vases and executing them in glass, precious metals, and decorated faience. They often embellished these vases with floral motifs.

The Greeks enlivened their assemblies by carpeting the floors of the buildings where they were held with scented rose petals. In their mythology they were fond of flower themes. Occasionally gods would appear in floral, rather than human, form. Iris, the messenger of the gods, was let down from heaven on a bridge that was a rainbow. Narcissus, who pined away for the love of his own image, which he saw reflected in a pool of water, was transformed into the flower that still bears his name. Hyacinthus, a handsome, well-loved young man, was accidentally killed by Apollo; and the blood from his mortal wound made the hyacinth grow.

What we typically think of as an English flower arrangement—large, lush, irresistibly beautiful, and made for spacious and comfortable country houses—was pioneered by the Victorians in the late nineteenth century. They loved informal, exuberant, and romantic bouquets with tall stems and much mixing of floral types, colors, and textures. Indeed, their bouquets were very like the grand arrangements Giftos creates each week for the Metropolitan's Great Hall.

Also during the nineteenth century, avid flower collectors, striving to satisfy their lust for the new, the exotic, and the spectacular, brought plants to the United States from South America, Africa, and China. At the same time, knowledgeable amateurs were busy writing books on flower arranging, which were eagerly devoured by a public that could not get enough of the subject. Women's magazines were brimming with tips on the display and care of flowers, both cut in the garden and purchased from shops. The profession of florist developed as yet one more way to satisfy the insatiable demand.

In the buttoned-up, straitlaced Victorian era, flowers became secret codes for expressing feelings that might seem too risqué or confrontational to speak about. Receiving a bouquet of yellow roses was not a happy event for those who understood the code because the yellow rose signified jealousy and a decrease in love. When long boxes filled with La France roses arrived at the door, hearts began to flutter because the sender was hinting boldly that the lady he was pursuing should meet him by moonlight. Changing the color of the same flower from week to week could raise or lower the stakes significantly. For example, if the yellow acacia in this week's delivery was a substitute for the white acacia in last week's, the symbolism had shifted dramatically from chaste love to secret love. This kind of floral game-playing surely added spice to the publicly restricted lives of Victorian ladies. However, one cannot help wondering how many Victorian gentlemen actually took the time and trouble to memorize the appropriate code.

But whatever flowers did or did not mean in code was merely a playful and quaint trifle, like the puns of which the English are so fond. The important point then, as now, is enjoyment. Flowers are one of the great delights of life, whether growing in the backyard, appearing as if by magic in the seasonally planted islands running up the center of New York City's Park Avenue, thriving in window boxes, or showing off in the lofty Great Hall of the Metropolitan. They give a world of pleasure to everyone who sees them, smells them, or touches them. If someone is in love, bringing an armload of specially chosen flowers to his or her beloved is an instinctive way to express it; if someone has made a terrible gaffe, it is flowers that are sent as the messengers of contriteness and apology; if someone gets sick or has an operation, again it is flowers to the rescue. At births, weddings, and funerals, it's flowers, flowers, and more flowers.

We take great joy in the beauty of flowers and are thankful that nature has provided us with this richness, comfort, and uncomplicated loveliness. Watching flowers reappear each spring reinforces our hope for the future, our dream of immortality. In a private house, flowers add graciousness and feelings of gaiety, warmth, and exhilaration that enrich our lives. Nature in the shape of flowers comes indoors like a blithe spirit to take up impermanent residence among us, embellishing our rooms along with the furniture, art, objects, and people.

And so at the Metropolitan Museum, rare and precious flowers live in perfect harmony with great art and spectacular settings. The Met deserves the special place it holds in the hearts of its visitors, who feel so warmly welcomed and appreciated. The flowers set the tone. They transform each visit into a festive occasion.

CHAPTER ONE

THE TEMPLE OF DENDUR IN THE SACKLER WING

Right and overleaf:

The two-thousand-year-old Egyptian temple is viewed across a reflecting pool that symbolizes the Nile, beside which it was originally built around 15 B.C. Giftos brings the complex to life with exuberant, towering bouquets of banana palm fronds and purple wild onions. "Delicate arrangements would have gotten lost next to such bold architecture," says Giftos.

❧ BATHED IN NATURAL LIGHT, THE ANCIENT EGYPTIAN Temple of Dendur in the Sackler Wing has been reerected at the Metropolitan Museum in a setting created to approximate the rocky desert landscape of Nubia (now Egypt), where the temple was originally built around 15 B.C. on the banks of the Nile. A U-shaped reflecting pool, planted with papyruslike reeds, represents the Nile. The temple and its tall, massive gateway sit on a platform that simulates the ancient river site. To reach the temple and gate, visitors climb wide granite steps, which demarcate the architectural complex from the sculpture court surrounding it.

Dedicated to the goddess Isis, the temple also honors two deified brothers, Pedesi and Pihor, sons of a local Nubian ruler who had sided with the Roman emperor Augustus in the struggle against the ruling queen of Meroe farther south. The temple was built in the name of Augustus, who, as ruler of Egypt after the battle of Actium, was represented as a pharaoh on the stone carvings of the temple's walls.

In considering flowers for the temple, Chris Giftos searched for "blooms that made a statement," and that are "as tall and powerful as the temple." His choices include bold red flowering ginger and long, pointed foxtail lilies. He also looked for foliage that "would have danced in the breezes that blew across the desert at night." Feathered banana palm fronds and graceful purple-headed flowering wild onions met his criteria. Giftos grouped them in "arrangements of pure fantasy to go with the fantastic architecture."

Dedicated to the goddess Isis and honoring two Nubian princes, the temple was home to the gods, according to Egyptian tradition. Only priests, who served the gods, could enter it. The magnificent facade is punctuated by two columns with papyrus-leaf capitals. Most of the rich, stylized carvings on the facade depict the Roman emperor Caesar Augustus offering gifts to Isis, the deified princes, and several Nubian gods. To complement the noble and highly embellished facade, Giftos creates twelve-foot-high floral columns with red flowering ginger, feathered banana palms, and cone-shaped foxtail lilies.

The temple gate is "a perfect frame for a massive arrangement," says Giftos. Here, bright purple wild onions are set off by tropical greens. Flowers and plants are integral to the decorative temple carvings. Near the base of the gateway, a stand of papyrus is incised in the stone.

Opposite:

Massive stone statues, dating from the fourteenth century B.C., represent the Egyptian pharaoh Amenhotep III. During his forty-year reign, he commissioned the renowned Luxor Temple. Originally, the statues flanked one of the gateways. Here, they have been positioned in front of the Dendur gate, on the opposite side of the reflecting pool. Giftos, not wanting to detract from their mysterious grandeur, simply floats in the pool a cluster of delicate papyrus, whose finely tufted tops catch the spirit of the delicate stone carvings.

The temple stands on a platform that recalls its ancient site along the Nile. Here, in a landscape of neutral grays and beiges like that of the Nubian desert, Giftos interjects "a shot of lively color." In his lush yet delicate floral arrangement, he juxtaposes purple wild onions with a flurry of white dogwood, yellow foxtail lilies, and wild grasses. "The dogwood and wild grasses soften the mix," explains Giftos. To the right of the bouquet is a headless Egyptian statue from the Ptolemaic Period (2nd–1st century B.C.).

"I found the lotus pods and the papyrus in the flower market, and the whole arrangement became very Egyptian," says Giftos. Sunny yellow billyballs and lavender agapanthus cheer up the mix. Incised in the stone wall is the figure of Caesar Augustus offering gifts to Isis.

CHAPTER TWO

THE WRIGHTSMAN GALLERIES

You could say that fragrance is the theme of this salon from the Hôtel de Cabris, which was built in the 1770s in the town of Grasse, the center of the French perfume industry. Gilded images of incense burners decorate the doors. Giftos enhances the space with aromatic flowers: Pungent lilies, stock, and lisianthus bedeck the mantelpiece, which is fronted by a gilded beechwood firescreen made in 1786 by Georges Jacob for Marie Antoinette's boudoir at the Château de Fontainebleau. Charming little bouquets of roses and lilies of the valley, typical of the period, are placed on small tables. Giftos's delicate color choices echo the pale palette of the room.

❧ THE WRIGHTSMAN GALLERIES CONTAIN THE FINEST collection in America of eighteenth-century French decorative arts, spanning the reigns of Louis XIV (reigned 1643–1715) and Louis XVI (reigned 1774–1792). The furniture and objets d'art in the sumptuous period rooms are exquisite examples of the lavish aristocratic taste of the period, typified by jeweled snuffboxes, porcelain objects, gilded seat furniture, and lacquered writing desks. The walls in these rooms are covered in painted and often gilded oak paneling that was specially made for houses in Paris, Grasse, and Vienna.

Among the period rooms are several salons, which are large and elaborate chambers from grand eighteenth-century French town houses (or *hôtels*). One salon was originally made for the Hôtel de Tessé (1768–72), a private house in Paris overlooking the Seine. The salon's carved Neoclassical paneling (attributed to Nicolas Huyot), both sober and delicate, is notable for its laurel sprays around the mirrors and other floral details.

Another late-eighteenth-century room came from the Hôtel de Cabris in Grasse, twelve miles from the seaside resort of Cannes. The cool, formal salon was created for a marquis and his wife and features painted and gilded paneling in the Louis XVI style. It is fitting that the doors are detailed with images of stately incense burners because Grasse is the center of France's perfume industry. Trophies depicting musical instruments can be seen in the corners of this quintessentially Neoclassical room.

The paneling in the Louis XV gallery, featuring musical instruments and theatrical masks, is a playful backdrop for a grand portrait of Louis XV (1710–1774) as a child, sitting majestically with a white ermine cape over his shoulders. Painted by Hyacinthe Rigaud (c. 1715–24), it is a regal, yet personal, glimpse of the young king.

The Palais Paar room comes from a Baroque palace in Vienna, built in about 1630 for Baron Johann Christoph von Paar, postmaster of the Holy Roman Empire; Count Wenzel Johann Joseph von Paar remodeled it in 1765–72.

The Hôtel de Varengeville was built in Paris in 1704 for the widowed marquise de Varengeville and remodeled in 1736–52. Its Rococo salon, installed at the museum, is a grand reception room with paneling enriched with carved and gilded decoration and large mirrors.

Delicate floral motifs abound in the so-called Sèvres room, which contains remarkable examples of furniture decorated with Sèvres porcelain plaques. Their charming bouquet designs are a perfect complement to the Neoclassical motifs painted on the wall panels.

For Giftos, the challenge was how to accessorize these salons with flowers when they are already so sumptuously appointed. He decided to create "smaller floral arrangements than in the other period rooms or galleries because everything else is so ornate and grand, including the paintings, the gilding, and the size of the draperies." But "the flowers had to be of the highest quality," Giftos says, "since no expense was spared in the salons. You would not want to use gladioli or chrysanthemums here." Instead, he chose lisianthus, flaming parrot tulips, roses, and lilies of the valley.

Opposite:

Abouquet of dusty pink roses, long sensuous calla lilies, dainty sprays of didiscus, and sprightly blue tweedia sits on a small writing table decorated with marquetry of tulipwood, kingwood, holly, and purplewood by Roger Van der Cruse Lacroix (c. 1765).

Left:

Late-eighteenth-century French decorative arts were extremely refined and highly luxurious, as shown in a rare gilt-bronze and openwork ivory urn and a mahogany side table richly mounted with gilt bronze (1785–90) by Jean-Henri Riesener. This sensibility is deftly captured by Giftos's lush bouquet: pale pink rhododendron, lavender didiscus, white ranunculus, purple hyacinth, and red yarrow.

A small, oval table by Martin Carlin (c. 1785), veneered with Japanese and European lacquer and ebony and finished in gilt bronze, accompanies a side chair of gilded beechwood. As a counterpoint to the luxurious furniture, Giftos creates a simple posy of white lilies of the valley and purple leucocoryne.

Opposite:

In the salon of the Hôtel de Cabris, Giftos displays a mass of lush pink azaleas on a gilded oak and beechwood incense burner.

A magnificent portrait (c. 1715–24) of Louis XV as a boy is reflected in a large mirror in the Louis XV gallery, which features wall panels depicting musical instruments and theatrical masks. The bouquet is a dramatic mix of purple agapanthus and calla lilies. Though bold in shape, the flowers are delicate in bloom, especially the petit-point white bridal rose sprays. "I chose them for their icy white and blue colors, which go with the wintry palette of the decor," Giftos says.

In this grand Parisian salon from the Hôtel de Varengeville, a small, vivacious bouquet of red and white flowers and variegated green-and-white leaves adds to the luster of the furnishings. Vivid amaryllis minerva mingle with fluted red calla lilies, bordeaux, and tiny spiky red celosia. Both the amaryllis and the calla lilies have long stems, which Giftos cut short so that "the focus is on their blooms, not their stems." Curving gilt-bronze candlesticks frame the robust bouquet on a 1759 writing table made by Giles Joubert for Louis XV's study at Versailles.

A rare eighteenth-century Chinese celadon vase with gilt-bronze mounts blends harmoniously with a bouquet of long-stemmed delphiniums, wild cherry branches, and flashes of white stock. "Just as the designer of the commode combined rich materials, I mixed up wildflowers, garden flowers, and hothouse flowers," says Giftos.

Flowers are a recurring theme in the Palais Paar room, appearing in the exquisite inlaid tables, the needlepoint screen, and the porcelain inkstand. "Floral illustration was popular in the Rococo period," says Giftos. He captures the delicacy of the table's floral marquetry, composed of mother-of-pearl, stained horn, and various woods, with a small, restrained bouquet of lilies of the valley ("a natural since the French love *muguet*") and purple salvia ("to pick up the blue in the porcelain").

Bright yellow sandersonia in a simple glass vase share a marble table-top with a candelabrum displaying a whimsical porcelain figure of a Chinese boy. An eighteenth-century Portuguese mandolin, inlaid with tortoise, ivory, and ebony, rests on a gilded armchair.

Left:

A strikingly unusual bouquet: Pale pink roses, chocolate cosmos, and mocha scabiosa are tucked into a container wrapped with variegated ivy. "Each flower can be savored individually," says Giftos. "They are not so crowded that you cannot appreciate each blossom." The earthy colors of a late-eighteenth-century terra-cotta sculpture of cavorting bacchanalian revelers echo the dusky tones in the floral arrangement, as does the brecciated marble top of the console table on which it is displayed.

"Flowers as delicate-looking as this ostrich egg vase" is Giftos's description of the sweet peas and ferns he chose. An inkwell and a candlestick of gilt bronze serve as handsome accompaniments on the marquetry writing table, made by master cabinet-maker Joseph Baumhauer about 1770.

Opposite:

Light and bright, the Sèvres room is filled with floral motifs. Bouquets are embroidered on the silk chair covers; Neoclassical urns with flowers are painted on the paneling; and colorful posies appear on the porcelain plaques that are inset in the furniture. "The decoration is lively and informal," says Giftos. "And you could say the same about the flower arrangements."

Left:

Hot pink anemones, red-and-white dahlias, and lipstick-pink gomphrena echo the feminine bouquets decorating a porcelain-fronted wood secretary (c. 1776).

Delicate green asparagus branches soften a vivid bouquet of lavender hydrangea and bright red celosia. "The colors in the arrangement pick up the vibrant shades of the paneling and Sèvres plaques," says Giftos. "The profusion of green branches and leaves heightens one's awareness of the forest-green porcelain trim on the bow-fronted secretary."

Left and overleaf:

Several objets d'art and pieces of furniture belonging to Marie Antoinette are found in the salon from the Hôtel de Tessé. The mechanical table (c. 1778), with marquetry of satinwood, purplewood, holly, and ebony, was used to serve her meals and hold her books and toiletries. It was made for the queen by Jean-Henri Riesener, who also made the ornate commode of ebony and Japanese lacquer and the matching secretary (out of view). Giftos chose flowers to echo the spirit of the elegant domestic furnishings— showy yellow-and-red striped flaming parrot tulips, proud chrome-yellow dahlias, and tiny blue delphiniums that flit like butterflies among the hothouse colors.

Full-blown Gertrude Jekyll roses make a glorious counterpoint to a cup, saucer, and creamer of Sèvres porcelain. Gilt-bronze tassels and rosettes embellish the Neoclassical table by Martin Carlin (c. 1780).

Opposite:

An eighteenth-century Chinese celadon vase mounted in a French gilt-bronze base perfectly complements a magnificent arrangement of pink bolero lilies, blue delphiniums, and cream Anna roses. The bust of the French philosopher Diderot was carved by Jean-Antoine Houdon in 1783. The front of the commode bears Marie Antoinette's monogram.

CHAPTER THREE

BLUMENTHAL PATIO

A midsummer night's dream: Garlands of gerbera and Queen Anne's lace wind exuberantly around marble columns in the Blumenthal Patio, a remarkable example of an Early Renaissance courtyard from a Spanish castle. A delicate white-and-green floral tableau complements the exquisite carvings. Giftos chose the palette, he says, because it is as "refined as the patio is elegant." Scores of white pear blossoms frame Tullio Lombardo's *Adam* (1490–95), one of the museum's Renaissance masterpieces. The effect is like a halo of baby's breath—light, airy, and graceful. Pruned and trained juniper tree topiaries and variegated ivy flank *Temperance*, a beautiful sixteenth-century sculpture of a woman meant to embody that virtue, by Giovanni Caccini.

The EARLY RENAISSANCE COURTYARD KNOWN AS THE Blumenthal Patio—with its two-story arcades of white marble, decorated with griffins and serpent-tailed birds—was originally built as part of an early-sixteenth-century castle in the remote Spanish town of Vélez Blanco. In the early twentieth century, it was transported to New York and installed in the Park Avenue mansion of George Blumenthal, one of America's most successful Gilded Age financiers. In its current incarnation at the museum, the patio serves as a gallery for Italian sculpture that boasts, among other treasures, Tullio Lombardo's *Adam* (1490–95), considered to be one of the museum's major Renaissance masterpieces.

Don Pedro Fajardo y Chacón, first marqués of Vélez, was the dashing young nobleman who built the patio. A Latin inscription carved in Roman capitals beneath the cornice in the courtyard reads:

> Pedro Fajardo, first marqués of Vélez and fifth governor of the kingdom of Murcia of his lineage, erected this castle as the castle of his title. This work was started in the year 1506 after the birth of Christ and finished in the year 1515.

Although the castle's architect is unknown, it is believed that the sculptors were Italians from Lombardy who had been invited to work on the nearby castle of La Calahorra (1509–12). The patio's arcades and Venetian-style window frames are decorated with a profusion of classical ornament, including foliate motifs, heraldic animals, trophies, shields, swords, musical instruments, and monsterlike creatures, such as griffins, leopards with curling serpent tails, and dolphins with curious whiskered human faces.

With the demise of the Fajardo line, Vélez Blanco passed to a new family. In 1904, the owners decided to remove the remaining furnishings from the apartments and to sell the richly carved patio. At that time, Renaissance architecture was in fashion among America's wealthy elite, having been championed by architects such as Stanford White and Charles Follen McKim. George Blumenthal, an investment banker and an art collector who was on the board of the Metropolitan Museum (and later its president), purchased the patio and made it the centerpiece of his mansion on the southwest corner of 70th Street and Park Avenue. The patio was covered with a coffered wooden ceiling, which had been removed from another part of the castle. Following Blumenthal's death, his house was demolished and the patio was dismantled and eventually rebuilt at the museum. Instead of the wooden ceiling, a glass roof was installed.

A patio such as this was meant to function as a court of honor, a place for pageantry, tournaments, and games. In keeping with this festive mood, at the museum today the Blumenthal Patio is a favorite place for parties, precisely because it is a lighthearted and joyful environment. "It is a great space for dancing," says Giftos, who always chooses celebratory flowers to decorate it. For one museum reception, he wound white rose and pear blossom garlands around the arches and balcony, as if creating a stage set for *A Midsummer Night's Dream*. "Throughout the years, people have used flowers to make celebratory garlands just as we use crepe paper today," Giftos says. On the tables, he centered boxwood topiaries "to give the effect of a Renaissance garden to match the Renaissance courtyard."

Opposite:

A plethora of white pear branches draws the eye to Tullio Lombardo's marble rendition of *Adam*. Garlands made of prince's pine are twined around the stately columns supporting the arcade. In the spandrels of the arcade can be seen the coat of arms of Don Pedro Fajardo y Chacón, the nobleman who built the patio in Vélez Blanco, Spain, starting in 1506.

Left:

A travertine and wrought-iron balcony from Italy on the second floor of the patio is romantically decorated with bouquets of tiny white roses and pink Peruvian lilies. The cascading blooms are complemented by swooping garlands of dark green prince's pine. Giftos's floral treatments are inspired by the imaginatively sculpted white marble arch and pilasters. The carvings depict flowers, bunches of fruit, dolphins with intertwining tails, and birds pecking at clusters of berries.

A pair of high-spirited griffins face off above an urn in a beautifully carved relief that decorates one of the tiered window frames in the Blumenthal Patio. As a counterpoint to the frenetic animal energy, Giftos juxtaposes a bouquet of great calm and purity, combining white Easter lilies and white Queen Anne's lace. He provides a shot of color with a few stalks of delphinium. Decorated with leaves, the vase is actually a medieval Spanish column capital that Giftos turned into a vase.

CHAPTER FOUR

ANNIE LAURIE AITKEN GALLERIES

J oyous swirls of stuccowork stand out against the straw-colored walls of the Kirtlington Park room.

♋ A STROLL THROUGH THE ANNIE LAURIE AITKEN Galleries makes you feel as if you have stepped into a grand British country house. The English period rooms at the Metropolitan Museum are widely regarded as the finest outside Britain, offering exquisite examples of Rococo and Neoclassical interiors and decorative arts. Within these period rooms, as well as in the galleries nearby, nearly eight hundred works of British art are displayed, including portraits by Romney and Wright of Derby, sculptures, rich tapestries, Baroque silver, and Wedgwood candlesticks.

At the entrance to the Aitken Galleries, there is a stately seventeenth-century staircase of lavishly carved oak, pine, and ash. Attributed to Edward Pearce, it originated in a manor house in Cassiobury Park, Hertfordshire, that had been owned by the Earl of Essex. Wonderful naturalistic carving decorates the stair rail; small birds perch on scrolls ending in pea pods, corn husks, and flowers. Wood pineapples, the traditional symbol of welcome, rest atop the newel posts.

Just off the stairhall is a room from Kirtlington Park, a Palladian-style manor house that was owned by Sir James Dashwood. The room was designed by John Sanderson and features flamboyant stuccowork executed by Thomas Roberts in 1744–45. Drawing on the Italian Baroque and the French Rococo styles, the plaster decoration displays an abundance of realistically rendered fruit and flowers. The extraordinary ceiling panels depict the four seasons; on the walls, life-size eagles grasp pendants of fruit and flowers in their talons.

Lansdowne House in Berkeley Square, London, was designed by the celebrated architect Robert Adam. Begun in 1761 for prime minister John Stuart and sold, unfinished, in 1765 to William Petty Fitzmaurice, the second earl of Shelburne and later the marquess of Lansdowne, the house was finally completed in 1769. The dining room (1766–69) displays Adam's characteristic Neoclassical style, inspired by the extensive excavations at Herculaneum and Pompeii in the 1740s and by the architect's 1757 visit to Diocletian's palace at Split, in Croatia. Ornament is expressed in cameolike motifs— rosettes, scrolls, trophies, and fans—and the subtle color palette creates an environment that is light, airy, and serene.

The staircase from Cassiobury Park and the rooms from Kirtlington Park and Lansdowne House offer the visitor a journey back to the era of the great English house. To enrich the experience, Giftos chose to lavish on the rooms "English bouquets that look as if the blooms came straight from the garden." They include typical country flowers: garden roses, green calla lilies, lavender, and mustard. His style departs somewhat from the more formal approach he used in the Wrightsman Galleries. The English bouquets may not be "as fussy as the French," says Giftos, "but each flower has its place."

Kirtlington Park, the house of Sir James Dashwood, was home to one of the Metropolitan's English period rooms, notable for its ornate Rococo stuccowork. Fruit, flowers, and birds depicted in plaster celebrate nature's bounty. Giftos contributes to this symphony of nature with a sumptuous arrangement of flowers framed by the splendid fireplace. "I was trying to create the illusion of a fire burning in the fireplace," says Giftos. "You look at the bouquet and you see flames of pink eupatorium with orange trumpet lilies and gold Teddy Bear sunflowers."

Opposite:

Serenely elegant, the Lansdowne House dining room (1766–69) was designed by the influential eighteenth-century architect Robert Adam, whose interiors are known for their delicate and refined Neoclassical motifs. Niches containing plaster copies of Roman and Greek statues embellish the walls.

Left and overleaf:

For this sumptuous and thoroughly modern flower arrangement, Giftos chose a lively mix of cotopaxi roses, mango calla lilies, delphinium belladonna, double French lilacs, white nigella, chocolate cosmos, yellow vallota, and crab apples. A magnificent array of English silver is on view: in the foreground, four candlesticks by Matthew Boulton (1806–08), and on the nearby side table, a hot-water urn and a pair of candlesticks by Thomas Heming (1772–73).

Luminous plaques dating from the seventeenth and eighteenth centuries have been fitted into a nineteenth-century cabinet (c. 1820–30) attributed to Robert Hume, a London cabinetmaker. Called *pietre dure* (literally "hard stones"), the flowery inlaid panels are composed of semiprecious stones, such as lapis lazuli, agate, and Sicilian jasper. The two side panels were made in the Grand Ducal workshops established by the Medici family in Florence, and the central plaque was possibly fabricated in Paris by the Gobelin workshops. Inspired by this exquisite tangle of fruit, flowers, and birds, Giftos creates a casual but stunning bouquet of ruby-colored paradise roses, yellow mustard, and orange gaillardia.

Giftos composes a startlingly original bouquet from plants that thrive in the shadowy depths of a garden: long fluted green calla lilies, puffy green viburnum, and the tailored green-and-white leaves of celathen. Tiny flashes of prunus enliven the mixture. The staircase of Cassiobury Park, a country house (demolished in 1920) in Hertfordshire, England, provides the perfect backdrop for his artistry. The unusual staircase (1677–80) is attributed to Edward Pearce. The stair rail is adorned with leafy tendrils and flowers, and pineapples sprout from the top of the newel posts.

CHAPTER FIVE

CARROLL AND MILTON PETRIE EUROPEAN SCULPTURE COURT

Designed to evoke the symmetry and formal arrangement characteristic of classical French gardens, the Carroll and Milton Petrie European Sculpture Court is a pleasant retreat within the museum. It is composed of parterres—geometric plots of greenery studded with statuary. On the north side is the exposed facade of the former carriage entrance to the Metropolitan Museum, designed in 1888 in the Renaissance Revival style. Front and center: a big, joyful arrangement of cherry blossoms, set off by areca palm fronds and trailing ivy. "It's a burst of color," says Giftos, "that brings the space to life."

The Carroll and Milton Petrie European Sculpture Court is not a traditional museum gallery, but a glass-enclosed sculpture garden inspired by the gardens at the seventeenth-century palace of Versailles. Created by the legendary landscape gardener André Le Nôtre, Versailles has "Gardens fit for gods," wrote the contemporary poet Jean de La Fontaine.

The vast palace and its complex of outbuildings, designed primarily by French architects Louis Le Vau and Jules Hardouin-Mansart and completed to a great extent between 1669 and 1685, included an Orangerie, whose design and surrounding landscaping inspired the Petrie Court. Louis XIV had a passion for collecting orange trees, sheltering as many as two thousand, in boxes, in his Orangerie during the winter. When spring came, gardeners moved the orange trees outdoors along the parterres (ornamental flower beds crisscrossed by pathways). Here, protected by two grand staircases and high walls, the orange trees bloomed and bore fruit.

In the Petrie Court, four parterres line the middle of the space. Framed with wood, the sections are painted green and planted with boxwood hedges and flowers. The south wall, a classical arcade, is loosely based on the facade of the Orangerie at Versailles. Ficus trees grow in tubs made by the same craftsmen who produce them for Versailles, where orange trees still grow today.

But the Petrie Court is not just a miniature Orangerie. Its north wall reveals the imposing Renaissance Revival–style facade of the former carriage entrance to the museum, built in 1888 as the museum's second wing. Bold and vigorous in its contrast of red brick and gray granite, it is a dramatic design. In the nineteenth century a grand stairway with two elaborate torchères led into the museum, and demonlike heads peered down at visitors from the cornice.

Most of the sculptures displayed in the courtyard were created for outdoor settings. There are sixteen pieces, eleven of which were made in the eighteenth century. Among them is the group called *The Allegory of the Elements* attributed to Jean-Pierre Defrance. Comprised of four women accompanied by putti, the group had decorated Mussegros, a château in Normandy. At the west end of the narrow courtyard are Rococo works, including *Fear of Cupid's Darts* (1739–40), a marble sculpture by Jean-Louis Lemoyne that depicts a mischievous cupid and a lively nymph. In the center of the court sits Jean-Antoine Houdon's figure of a young woman bathing, once placed in the duc de Chartres's Anglo-Chinese garden at Monceau, on the outskirts of Paris. The marble figure was originally set into a Neoclassical fountain grouping that consisted of the bather sitting in the middle of a basin accompanied by a female servant, cast in black lead, pouring water from a gilded ewer. Unfortunately, only the statue of the young maiden survives.

In front of the east wall, which is covered with ivy and latticework, are two striking sculptures, both carved in 1616 by Pietro Bernini with the help of his son Gian Lorenzo. One is a maiden holding a wicker basket overflowing with blooms; the other is a bearded man cradling a cornucopia of fruit in his arms. Created for Cardinal Scipione Borghese in Rome, the sculptures were placed at the main entrance to the Villa Borghese.

At Versailles and other European palaces, gardens often served as settings for grand fêtes, featuring dancing and music, even carousels and theater. With a similarly exuberant effect, Giftos arranges generous bouquets of pink cherry branches—ten feet high and twelve feet wide—which burst out of oversized urns designed in 1742. These pedestaled vases were commissioned to decorate the formal parterres in the gardens of the Château de Choisy, a favorite residence of Louis XV. Giftos had to be lifted up by a cherry picker to work on his arrangements. The blossoms animate the space with energy and color—a suitable counterpoint to a regal garden.

Opposite:

The Petrie Court's two extraordinary urns were commissioned by Louis XV in 1742 for the gardens of Château de Choisy. Decorated with swags of vines and grapes, satyrs' heads, and Bacchantes, the pair of pedestaled vases allude to the seasonal pleasures of autumn. Here, they are filled to the brim with spring blossoms. Behind the vase at the east end are two marble figures (1616) by Pietro and Gian Lorenzo Bernini from Cardinal Scipione Borghese's villa in Rome. They welcome the visitor with baskets abundant in fruit and flowers.

Left:

An explosion of pink blossoms leads the eye to two charming eighteenth-century sculptures, each an eight-foot-tall figure of a woman representing the earth's bounty. They are part of a group of four sculptures called *The Allegory of the Elements,* attributed to Jean-Pierre Defrance.

CHAPTER SIX

THE AMERICAN WING

Right and overleaf:

The majestic facade of the Branch Bank of the United States (Martin E. Thompson, 1822–24), which once stood on Wall Street, makes an imposing backdrop for the Charles Engelhard Court. The centerpiece is the half-size model of a thirteen-foot-high sculpture of Diana, the Roman goddess of the moon and of hunting, which had been a weather vane atop the original Madison Square Garden building (1890, now demolished) designed by the architect Stanford White. The gilded bronze statue was created by the noted sculptor Augustus Saint-Gaudens (this version was cast in 1928 after the sculptor's death). To celebrate Diana's beauty, Giftos sets off a fireworks of yellow forsythia exploding out of late-nineteenth-century cast-iron urns.

The Metropolitan Museum mounted its first exhibition of American art in 1909, to rave reviews.

"Why, those ancestors of ours had taste equally if not surpassing ours," exclaimed Lewis Mumford, the *New York World* art critic. "It is not merely an exhibition of art, it is a pageant of American history. Nothing so complete and tactful has ever been accomplished by an American museum."

By the early 1920s, there was growing enthusiasm and support among museum officials, patrons, and trustees for the idea of opening a special wing devoted to American art and design. In 1924, the imposing Neoclassical facade of New York City's Branch Bank of the United States (Martin E. Thompson, 1822–24) was salvaged from Wall Street and installed as the entrance to the new American Wing. Behind the bank facade were three floors of Colonial and Federal period rooms. Following more than five decades of acquiring American art, the museum undertook an ambitious project to expand the American Wing in the 1970s. Today, the wing contains twenty-five period rooms, ranging from a colonial hall (built before 1674) to a living room (1912–14) designed by Frank Lloyd Wright, America's most famous architect.

The entrance to the American Wing is a bright, glass-enclosed garden court. Called the Charles Engelhard Court, the space contains a reflecting pool, a fountain, and plantings composed of topiary trees in teak containers. Visitors can observe nineteenth- and twentieth-century sculptures scattered around the garden. The gleaming golden figure of the goddess Diana shooting a bow and arrow, by Augustus Saint-Gaudens, is a smaller version of the weather vane that once perched atop the original Madison Square Garden building (1890), designed by Stanford White.

At one end of the courtyard, opposite the bank facade, stands a colorful loggia glittering with iridescent tiles designed by Louis Com-

At one end of the vast court is the loggia from Laurelton Hall (c. 1904), which was the Long Island house of Louis Comfort Tiffany, son of Charles Lewis Tiffany, the founder of Tiffany & Company in New York. Best known for his exquisite glass designs, including leaded-glass windows and lamps, Louis Comfort Tiffany was also famous for jewelry, enamels, metalwork, and pottery. The capitals of the columns are ringed with ceramic poppies, peonies, lotus, and magnolia blossoms in three stages of bloom. Tiny pieces of green glass comprise the stems.

fort Tiffany. The copper-plated staircase from the Chicago Stock Exchange building (1894) was designed by another of America's renowned architectural geniuses—and Wright's teacher—Louis Sullivan.

One steps through the front doors of the bank facade to enter the galleries of the American Wing. The earliest period room is the Hart Room, built before 1674 in Ipswich, Massachusetts. The multi-purpose room was used for living, cooking, eating, and even sleeping. A wide fireplace dominates the space, and the ceiling, framed by heavy beams, was kept low to contain heat. The carved oak and pine furniture is characteristic of the simplicity of design in seventeenth-century America. An infusion of color is provided by the sunflowers and purple catnip in Giftos's bouquets. "I feel that they could have come straight from the Harts' garden," he says.

A world—and a century—away from the Hart Room in both mood and style is a gracious gallery with architectural details dating from the Federal period, which lasted from after the Revolution to about 1820. Known as the Phyfe Gallery, this bright interior boasts examples of Duncan Phyfe's elegant furniture, in addition to pieces by his contemporaries. Giftos's bouquets complement the graceful lines of the furniture. A magnificent arrangement—artichokes, magnolias, and dahlias—sits atop a Duncan Phyfe pier table. "I was looking for richness in style as well as in color and scent," says Giftos.

By the middle of the nineteenth century, Victorian taste favored an ornate, French-inspired aesthetic for furnishings and objets d'art. Furniture was curvaceous and robust in form; carpets vibrated with color; and windows were elaborately draped. Dating from about 1852, the American Wing's Rococo Revival parlor showcases this flamboyant style, typified by a suite of rosewood furniture by the German-born designer John Henry Belter. Flowers, grapes, vines, leaves, and snaky tendrils run rampant over the sofa, armchairs, side chairs, and table. In this room Giftos conducts a loud floral symphony of blue and white. The bouquet, full of long-stemmed campanula bellflower and fuchsia winter berries, is a nervous confection of tiny blossoms. His massing of blooms, which almost hide the marble top of the rosewood table, is in keeping with the aesthetic of the period.

In the elegant Renaissance Revival parlor from the residence of manufacturer Jedediah Wilcox, built in 1868–70 in Meriden, Connecticut, the style is rich and grand. The ceiling is painted and gilded with stenciled patterns and trompe l'oeil bouquets of flowers. A color scheme of tan walls and crimson draperies is enriched by sumptuous details such as the marble fireplace mantel and the carved mother-of-pearl medallions set into the rosewood seat backs, the overmantel mirror, and the window cornices. To go with this lavish setting, Giftos chose luscious pink hydrangea and red astilbe for the Egyptian Revival table. "I wanted flowers that are exuberant," he says. "A mix of textures is important—velvety roses, feathery astilbe, ruffled hydrangea, and silky-smooth cosmos."

Frank Lloyd Wright's living room from the Mr. and Mrs. Francis W. Little house in Wayzata, Minnesota, built in 1912–14, was created with nature in mind. He designed windows on all four walls so that natural views enhanced the room. Leaded-glass windows filter light as if through a canopy of trees. Wright borrowed from nature for structural and decorative elements: the horizontal thrust of rock ledges inspired his cantilevered walls; he abstracted the delicate reedy profile of prairie grass in leaded-glass motifs. Giftos chose a rustic style for his arrangements in the Frank Lloyd Wright room. "In addition to flowers, there are plenty of leaves, vines, and branches with berries," he says. "The colors are earthy to go with the warm golds and reddish-browns of the room."

Louis Comfort Tiffany created this mosaic landscape and fountain (c. 1905–15), an intricate and beautiful tableau of swans gliding on a pond in the foreground with a garden and sky in the background. A grouping of hot-pink cyclamen, protea, aralia, sego palms, raphis palms, rubber plants, Chinese fan palms, and Chinese evergreens adds another dimension to his rendition of nature.

"Welcome to the guest who arrives; farewell and helpfulness to him who departs" is a translation of part of the Latin inscription over this fireplace mantel, which originally dominated the entrance hall of Cornelius Vanderbilt's palatial house on Fifth Avenue and 57th Street in New York City. Sculptor Augustus Saint-Gaudens created the two marble caryatids, Amor (love) and Pax (peace). In keeping with the size and magnificence of the fireplace, Giftos shapes a generous bouquet of shiny green magnolia leaves, coppery scarlet oak leaves, and red cockscomb. He chose the colors to complement the bronze of the fireplace.

Playful, colorful, and cheerful, these stained-glass windows (c. 1912) are among Frank Lloyd Wright's most famous. He designed them in primary colors with balloonlike circles and confettilike squares for the Avery Coonley playhouse in Riverside, Illinois. Giftos distills their spirit with a happy-go-lucky parade of flowering purple wild onions, spiky purple agapanthus, yellow field daisies, and white gerbera.

A charming summer bouquet of sunflowers, purple catnip, and delicate yellow dill makes a perfect foil for the carved oak chest and handsome cradle in the Hart Room, a three-hundred-year-old colonial hall and the earliest of the American Wing period rooms.

This pure and formal Federal-style gallery showcases a wonderful set of dining furniture by Duncan Phyfe. Elegant Federal furniture is distinguished by stylized classical motifs such as lyres and garlands. A mirror edged in gilded wood (c. 1795) reflects a tumultuous bouquet of artichoke heads, magnolia seed pods, white dahlias, and purple larkspur. "The heady opulence of early New York was my inspiration here," says Giftos.

The curveaceous lines of the Rococo Revival style were popular in the mid-nineteenth century. The furniture is elaborately carved; the carpet is overrun with roses; and the windows are swagged and draped with tasseled fabrics.

This rosewood table, designed by John Henry Belter, is embellished with grape leaves, grape clusters, and vinelike tendrils. A sumptuous blue-and-white floral arrangement echoes the extravagance of the decoration. Giftos includes magic blue iris and purple veronica, mixing them with a dash of hot-pink gomphrena and snow-white winter berries.

Opposite and above:

This elegant Renaissance Revival parlor came from the Jedediah Wilcox house, built in 1868–70 in Meriden, Connecticut. Rich decorative elements include gilded sphinx heads on the Egyptian Revival rosewood table, the carved rosewood overmantel mirror and window cornices, and bright red curtains. Giftos accentuates the palette of the room with two bouquets based on red roses. In one, he softens the intensity of the red in the cotopaxi roses and the spiky astilbe with pink hydrangeas and white dahlias. In the other, he spices up the roses by adding astilbe, boisterous dahlias, and a smattering of hypericum berries.

Frank Lloyd Wright's living room from the Mr. and Mrs. Francis W. Little house, built in 1912–14 in Wayzata, Minnesota, was conceived as an almost freestanding pavilion with windows on all four sides. Wright revered nature and thought of architecture as its foil. To honor Wright's preference for casually arranged flowers, Giftos weaves a tangle of pear branches, viburnum leaves, red Flamenco and orange Tom Pearce chrysanthemums, and firethorn berries. The glowing autumnal colors echo the warm earthy hues of the room.

Wright's simple but splendid brick fireplace makes a strong architectural backdrop for Giftos's controlled tumble of red Leonardis roses, croton leaves, and bittersweet berries atop an oak table. A Wright-designed copper urn on the floor in front of the fireplace holds a cluster of coppery pear branches. "It is one room in the museum where I would feel comfortable sitting, so the arrangements are more homey," Giftos says.

CHAPTER SEVEN

THE ASTOR COURT

The recurring theme of opposites—
yin (dark and soft) and yang
(bright and hard)—heightens the visual
drama of the Astor Court. A proces-
sion of bright pink flowers directs
the eye around the perimeter of the
courtyard.

118

❧ THROUGH A CIRCULAR DOORWAY—CALLED A MOON gate—visitors to the Astor Court enter a wondrous Chinese garden courtyard, typical of those that flowered during the Ming dynasty. The spare, serene space reproduces a part of one of the most beautiful surviving gardens in China, Wang Shi Yuan (the Garden of the Master of the Fishing Nets). It was originally built in the southern Chinese city of Suzhou, on a site first used for a garden in the twelfth century. Still home to twenty elaborate gardens considered to be the finest examples of Ming garden architecture in China, Suzhou inspired the proverb, "In heaven is paradise; on earth is Suzhou."

The Chinese believe that change is the only constant aspect of existence. The Astor Court is a metaphor for that philosophy. A zigzagging covered walkway encourages visitors to see fresh and changing perspectives of a half pavilion to the left and a moon-viewing terrace beyond. A close look reveals that the spacing between the pillars of the walkway is irregular and that each example of geometric latticework covering the windows has a different design. Even the plants and trees are symbols of change. Neither clipped nor pruned nor planted in rows or rectangular beds, they grow as in the wild. Full of surprises and irregularities, the courtyard is a visual delight.

The ordering principle of the courtyard is yin and yang, complementary opposites that offer contrast and change. In nature, yin is cool, moist, dark, soft, and yielding; yang is characterized by strength, hardness, resistance, and light. In the Astor Court, yin and yang are expressed through the alternation of light and shadow, and in the subtle complexities of the design.

The Astor Court is as spiritual as a cathedral of pine trees. Visitors speak in whispers. They slow their gait to a stroll, stop, sit on stone stools, and observe the shadows of birds flying over the enormous glass skylight. They enjoy peering at the goldfish in a tiny pool, which gives the illusion that it bubbles up from an underground spring. The courtyard is not only a place of solace but also of sweet fragrances from a gathering of seasonal blossoms.

In China's history, courtyards have functioned as social centers as well as solitary retreats, where artists, inspired by beautiful flowers and fine food and wine, might gather. The Astor Court has served a similar function over the years, and Chris Giftos has created flower arrangements for such festive occasions. "We take a serene space and make it very pretty and soothing to the eye," he says. For a dinner celebrating the tenth anniversary of the courtyard's completion, he filled the space with pastel-colored lilacs, sweet peas, and roses—all blooms with dainty petals and delicate scents. "I look for subtle arrangements with less color variation because the space is small [fifty-nine by forty feet] and quiet. It would be overwhelmed by immense bouquets," he says.

It took a team of twenty-seven craftsmen and engineers from Suzhou six months to complete the Astor Court. After returning home, they wrote to Brooke Astor, the courtyard's benefactor: "We put our hearts and our spirits into our work for you, and our friendship will flourish forever like an evergreen tree." It was always Mrs. Astor's hope that a visit to the courtyard would be a spiritual and rewarding experience.

Two tall *Cymbidium* orchids stand like gaudily uniformed sentinels, along with a fierce stone lion (a genuine Ming Dynasty statue), one of a pair that guards the Astor Court. The entrance portal, known as a moon gate, frames a vista into the courtyard. The Chinese characters in relief on the ceramic tablet above the gate mean "In Search of Quietude." Giftos does his part to soothe the eye by massing pink azaleas in a simple wooden box. A lacy Chinese latticed window affords glimpses of bamboo and palm trees beyond.

After stepping through the moon gate, visitors follow a covered pathway, hugging the periphery of the courtyard, to splendidly crafted lattice-work doors that open into a scholar's study. The zigzag course of the pathway is meant to encourage them to walk slowly, turning this way and that, enjoying new vistas. Giftos tucks a surprise here and there—a pot of white *Phalaenopsis* (moth) orchids on the pathway railing, a small forest of astilbe filling a niche. In the background are the pale pink blossoms of *Cymbidium* orchids. These dainty blooms complement the finely grained *nan* wood pillars, carved by hand from hundred-year-old trees and polished to a rich dark sheen.

Left:

The traditional Chinese garden pavilion has upturned eaves and terra-cotta roof tiles that are marked with the symbols for long life, wealth, and happiness. This architectural gem houses a reproduction blue-and-white Ming vase filled with cherry blossoms. "The arrangement is free-form," says Giftos, "to complement the informality of the Chinese garden." A banana palm, a ficus tree, azaleas, and *Cymbidium* orchids are planted amid exotically shaped limestone rocks, meant to encourage the travel of the imagination.

CHAPTER EIGHT

THE CLOISTERS

Right and overleaf:

The Langon Chapel incorporates interior stonework that was originally part of the south wall of the choir from a twelfth-century church south of Bordeaux, as well as a twelfth-century Romanesque wooden sculpture of the *Enthroned Virgin and Child* and thirteenth-century French stained-glass windows. The bouquet contains Eucharist lilies, irises, and sweet william, none of them medieval species but chosen by Giftos because they convey a sense of the period.

The Unicorn in Captivity. Franco-Flemish, c. 1500. Silk, wool, silver, and silver-gilt threads. H 12' 1" x W 8' 3". The Metropolitan Museum of Art. Gift of John D. Rockefeller, Jr., The Cloisters Collection, 1937

AT THE NORTHERN TIP OF MANHATTAN, ON A HILLTOP in Fort Tryon Park, stands a branch of the Metropolitan Museum known as The Cloisters. Visitors follow a winding road to reach weathered granite ramparts at the entrance to what appears to be a medieval monastery, with a Romanesque bell tower and chapels with red-tile roofs and stained-glass windows.

Opened in 1938, this twentieth-century structure was artfully designed in a style evocative of medieval monasteries and castles and, in fact, incorporates sections from a twelfth-century chapter house, cloisters from five medieval French monasteries, and two Romanesque chapels. "It is a jewel in the city," Giftos says. "When people come here they are amazed at how immersed they feel in the medieval world."

Inside The Cloisters, among the many treasures, is the prized tapestry series illustrating The Hunt of the Unicorn (c. 1500), and a comprehensive collection of medieval sculpture, ivories, reliquaries, manuscripts, and other works of art. The cloister gardens from the monasteries of Bonnefont-en-Comminges, Trie-en-Bigorre, and Saint-Michel-de-Cuxa contain one of the most unusual plant collections in the world, with more than 250 species used in the Middle Ages.

The Bonnefont Cloister, which affords a spectacular view of the Hudson River, contains a remarkable herb garden. All the plants growing there have a practical application. In the Middle Ages, such plants were used for seasonings, medicines, scents, cosmetics, and dyes. Flax, which was spun for the thread used in medieval tapestries, can also be found among the herbs. Nineteen raised flower beds surround a fifteenth-century Venetian well head, and quince trees, popular for their large golden fruit, are planted in the center of the garden.

The Trie Cloister garden is based on the many varieties of plants depicted in the Unicorn tapestries, which feature a Gothic garden with a central fountain where birds come to drink.

Cuxa, the largest of the museum's cloisters, came from the Benedictine monastery of Saint-Michel-de-Cuxa in the northeastern Pyrenees. The Cuxa garden is divided into quadrants, each with a floral edging and a fruit tree: hawthorn, crab apple, cornelian cherry, or pear. In order to ensure color from spring to fall, modern flowers are blended with the medieval species.

Giftos creates his own tapestry of color by choosing medieval as well as modern flowers for his bouquets. "What a wonderful sense of continuity to create a bouquet that might have been arranged hundreds of years ago," he says. "Lilies and roses, as well as herbs, were used in medieval festivals and rituals. They have such a history that you feel their power just holding them in your hands."

The Unicorn Tapestries (c. 1500), one of the most remarkable series of medieval tapestries in the world, depicts the hunt and capture of the unicorn, a legend that also had associations with courtly love and Christ's passion. The tapestries are renowned for their accurate renderings of plants and animals, all infused with symbolism. Red roses signify the charity and compassion of the Virgin Mary, who is represented by the maiden who tames the unicorn. The hawthorn tree was believed in the Middle Ages to be the tree from which Christ's crown of thorns was made. The pomegranate was a symbol of immortality and fertility. The captive unicorn is shown against a background called *millefleurs* (a thousand flowers), in which the plants and flowers are so perfectly executed that it is possible to distinguish each petal—even the veins of leaves, thorns, and other fine details.

A spectacular "tree" composed by Giftos stands to the side of the arches leading to the Bonnefont Cloister. The trunk, nestled in a mossy basket, is wrapped with grapevines. Twisted branches of cherry, crab apple, and viburnum erupt from the top. This fantasy creation is a brilliant burst of color, accentuated by the ascetic gray stone walls of the building.

The Bonnefont Cloister herb garden boasts approximately 250 culinary and medicinal herbs, fruits, and vegetables. The marble capitals and columns come from a Cistercian abbey at Bonnefont-en-Comminges and other monastic buildings southwest of Toulouse in southern France. Giftos felt that love-in-a-mist and lavender were perfectly suited to the medieval setting. "I asked one of the horticulturists to accompany me on a trip to the flower market and help me select flowers that would have grown in the Middle Ages, or would be in the spirit of the period," says Giftos. "I created very free-form arrangements—just loosely gathered—because they matched the relaxed mood of the garden."

Many of the plants that are depicted in the famous Unicorn Tapestries are planted in the lovely garden of the Trie Cloister. Marble capitals and columns, most from the Carmelite convent of Trie-en-Bigorre in southwestern France, frame a generous floral bouquet in a basket made of birch twigs. Giftos plays off summer field flowers—teasel, delicate Queen Anne's lace, and sea holly—against the cool stone. Like fireflies, tiny red wild roses brighten the mix.

ACKNOWLEDGMENTS

Richard R. Morsches, Senior Vice President for Operations at The Metropolitan Museum of Art, for his insight and trust in bringing me from Christatos and Koster and developing a new position for both me and the Museum

Philippe de Montebello, Director of The Metropolitan Museum of Art, for allowing me to create the fantasy

The curators and technicians from the departments of Egyptian Art, American Art, European Sculpture and Decorative Arts, Asian Art, Medieval Art, and The Cloisters for their permission, assistance, and guidance

The administration of the departments of Egyptian Art, American Decorative Arts, European Sculpture and Decorative Arts, Asian Art, Medieval Art, and The Cloisters, as well as the Watson Library and Archives, for their cooperation in providing information

Barbara Burn, for serving as an invaluable liaison between Abrams and the Museum staff

Kristin Perry, my Special Events Coordinator, for her devotion and dedication and for gathering information necessary to complete the text of this book

Butzi Moffitt, my one and only devoted volunteer, without whose commitment to this project would never have been completed

Efrain Aviles, whose heart is larger than the flower arrangements themselves, for his creativity and assistance in making my job possible

The Museum's buildings and gardening technicians George Spencer, Nicholas Mamatos, Gaspard Alexander, Paul Moy, and Paul Zaccagnimo, whose contribution of time and energy has enabled the world to enjoy the Museum's flowers and plants

Barbara Plumb, for her spirited and informative text, which perfectly complements the flowers

Page Starzinger, for her valuable background research

Alec Hemer, for capturing my flower arrangements so beautifully through his talent for photography and lighting

At Abrams, Elisa Urbanelli, for her skillful editing, and Darilyn Carnes, for her elegant book design

My friends at the flower market for keeping the Met in bloom

And finally, the millions of visitors from all over the world who come to the Metropolitan Museum and exclaim, "These are the most beautiful artificial flowers I have ever seen!"

C.P.G.